# YO

## NATIONAL

by

## DOUGLASS H. HUBBARD
### Former Chief Park Naturalist

Illlustrated by

## GEORGE SANDSTROM
and

## REBECCA MERRILEES

# WELCOME!

In 1864, during the Civil War, President Abraham Lincoln signed a bill which set aside Yosemite Valley and the Mariposa Grove of Giant Sequoias to be kept for your enjoyment---"inalienable for all time." It was the first action of this kind in the world.

In those days getting to Yosemite was both an adventure and a hardship over nearly impassable roads and trails. Today you can drive to the park in air-conditioned comfort over scenic mountain highways.

But don't stay in your car---take a free bus ride around Yosemite Valley, a nature walk with a park ranger, or go to an evening campfire program. The National Park Service provides a variety of activities for your enjoyment. There is something for every taste and pocket book: Junior Rangers for the youngsters, free shuttle busing, cowboy-led trail rides, river rafting, mountain climbing school, free art classes in summer, and skiing, snow-boarding and ice skating in winter. Check at an information desk, bulletin board or read the park newspaper to find out what's going on and where.

Above all, enjoy your park---it is unique in the world. In addition to magnificent cliffs and waterfalls you'll see Giant Sequoia trees, tiny chipmunks and beautiful wildflowers living together as they have done for countless ages. They all belong to you so take care of them.

You may wish to join the Yosemite Association. Since 1923 this non-profit educational organization has been dedicated to the support of Yosemite National Park through a program of visitor services, publications, and membership activities. For more information write Post Office Box 230, El Portal, CA. 95318, phone (209) 379-2646, or e-mail www.yosemite.org.

# CONTENTS

## UNIQUE YOSEMITE

Nowhere in the world has nature been more lavish with beauty than in Yosemite. Here you see granite in immense rounded domes or in sheer cliffs with waterfalls plunging thousands of feet to the valley below. Here, too, are the Giant Sequoias, the largest of all living things. Cascades level into mirror-clear meadow streams and lakes; sunsets paint the canyons with a riot of color. These spectacular features have made Yosemite world-famous.

From Glacier Point you can see Nevada and Vernal falls and hear the Merced River thundering down the Giant Stairway. Half Dome, Yosemite's most famous dome, rises to the left.

Forsyth Peak

Matterhorn Peak

Lake Eleanor

Hetch Hetchy Reservoir

Mt Conness

Tuolumne River    Water Wheel Falls

Tioga Pass

Tuolumne Meadows Lodge

White Wolf Lodge

Mt Dana

Big Oak Flat Entrance

May Lake

Tenaya Lake

Mono Pass

Yosemite Falls

Tuolumne Grove

Merced Grove    Yosemite Valley    Half Dome

High Sierra Loop Trail

Mt Lyell

Arch Rock Entrance    Merced River    Glacier Point Overlook

Badger Pass Ski Area

Fernandez Pass

N

Pioneer Yosemite History Center

Mariposa Grove Lodge & Museum

South Entrance Rt.

## YOSEMITE NATIONAL PARK

Regardless of what season you choose your visit will be more complete if you study the maps and guides you have received. These will help you decide what you want to see and do.

This guide, the National Park Service literature detailing daily activities, and roadside signs and exhibits explain park features and will help you make the best use of your time.

To Lower Yosemite Fall

Lower Yosemite Fall

U.S. Court

Yosemite Falls Trail

Columbia Rock

Camp 4

YOSEMITE VILLAGE

Yosemite Museum and Indian Village
Ansel Adams Gallery

Park Headquarters

Wilderness Center W

Post Office

Medical Clinic

Village Store

Auto repair

The Ahwahnee

Self-guiding trail

Sentinel Bridge

P Day-use parking

Indian Canyon Creek

Yosemite Creek

Yosemite Lodge

Merced River

Housekeeping Camp

Camp...

Chapel

Stoneman Bridge

LeConte Memorial Lodge

Curry Villa

Bridge 4

Union Point

Moran Point

Staircase Falls

Four Mile Trail (summer only)

Sentinel Creek

Sentinel Rock
7038ft
2145m

Sentinel Fall

Pohono Trail

Sentinel Dome
8122ft
2476m

Sentinel Dome Trail

Glacier Point Road
(closed November to May)

To Taft Point

G
(su
72
21

Yosemite Valley Visitor Center

# The Incomparable Yosemite Valley

Maps courtesy of the National Park Service

**Lyell Glacier on Mt. Lyell**

**THE HIGH SIERRA** of Yosemite—the glaciers such as Lyell, alpine meadows and lakes, snow-covered peaks—is seldom seen by visitors. The park ranges in elevation from 2,000 ft. near the Arch Rock Entrance to more than 13,000 ft. at the top of Mt. Lyell.

**Hanging Gardens on Mt. Dana**

**THE HANGING GARDENS** on the slopes of Mt. Dana near Tioga Pass (10,000 ft.) are splashes of bright color toward the end of August or early September. The scenery varies from parched foothills up the mountain to meadows and hillsides in full bloom.

**TUOLUMNE MEADOWS**, the largest alpine meadow in the Sierra, may be reached in summer by the Tioga Road. Ranger-naturalists lead hikes over high country trails that begin here.

**Mt. Gibbs, near Tioga Pass**

**CAMPGROUNDS** in various parts of the park are often cooler, less-crowded than in Yosemite Valley. Park publications show locations. Backpackers must use assigned camp sites.

**VISITORS** who cannot go to the High Sierra may get a breathtaking view of Yosemite Valley and a glimpse of the high country beyond Half Dome from Glacier Point. Visitors hiking into the back country should discuss their plans with a ranger.

**View toward High Sierra**

**ROCKS** form the scenery of Yosemite. The valley was carved from a great block of granite and owes its beauty to this durable igneous rock. Differing mineral content and speed of cooling formed a dozen varieties, all extremely hard. In the Merced River Canyon, below the park, are tilted beds of gray slate, originally mud, the remnants of ancient sea bottoms. Yosemite's oldest rocks are there, too—folded masses of greatly changed sediments that were pushed aside by rising granite. Near the crest of the Sierra are rust-red peaks of quartzite made from sandstone that was metamorphosed by the heat and pressure that formed the Sierra Nevada.

**GRANITES** are rocks formed from molten magma within the earth's crust. As the rock minerals cooled, they formed interlocking crystals of quartz, feldspar and mica, or other dark mineral. Each new uprising of magma in Yosemite formed a granite of slightly different composition and appearance.

Yosemite granites range from speckled white to mottled gray, and from fine to coarse grained. The peaks, domes and the valley itself are made of granite. The granites in Yosemite are often named for the famous features they form, as Cathedral Peak granite, El Capitan granite, and Sentinel Peak granite.

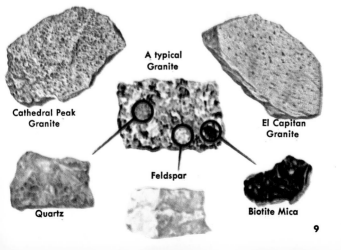

A typical Granite

Cathedral Peak Granite

El Capitan Granite

Feldspar

Quartz

Biotite Mica

Other Yosemite rocks include several that are akin to granite. When a granitic magma cools very slowly, large crystals form and accessory minerals crystallize, and the rock formed is pegmatite. Pegmatites fill veins and fissures of the Yosemite granites. When less quartz is present, granites grade off into granodiorites and diorites. The diorites are dark rocks made up of feldspars and dark minerals such as hornblende and other dark silicates. Dikes or pegmatite and fine-grained aplite can be seen on the domes and walls of Yosemite Valley.

PEGMATITE fills veins and fissures in granite.

PEGMATITE in contact with dark diorite.

GRANODIORITE, a transition rock of Yosemite.

DIORITE is a dark igneous rock —contains no quartz.

BANDED QUARTZITE, an altered metamorphic sandstone.

GOLD does not occur in Yosemite but the gold-bearing mother lode is nearby. Placer mining came first; shaft mining was discontinued about 1940.

**THE SIERRA NEVADA**, the longest and highest mountain range in the U.S., is a tremendous block of granite, nearly 400 miles long and from 60 to 80 miles wide. Its slope to the west is gentle; to the east, it rises to more than 14,000 ft. The Sierra was formed in several stages. It began with deposits on the sea bottom. Then a great batholith of molten material pushed upward from deep in the earth, was worn down and raised again by several strong uplifts and westward tilting. Rivers and glaciers cut deeply to carve a rugged typography between remnants of older, previously eroded surfaces.

**UPLIFTING** and TILTING to the west changed the course of a number of streams to run directly down the west slope. The speed of their cutting was greatly accelerated. Faulting—the fracturing and displacement of the rock masses—followed the uplift along the eastern slope. In this period the Owens Valley block collapsed, forming a basin for Mono Lake. A warm climate followed the last of the glaciers, some 10,000 years ago. The small glaciers, as those of Mt. Lyell, Mt. Dana and Mt. Conness may represent remnants of former ice masses or may be new formations due to cooling within the last 3,000 years.

The Sierra Nevada in cross section, from the first uplift to today. 1. Granite has pushed up beneath the sedimentary rocks of the ancestral range. 2. Much of the old rock has been eroded and washed into the San Joaquin Valley. 3. The Sierra today, with Yosemite Valley on the west slope, Mono Lake to the east.

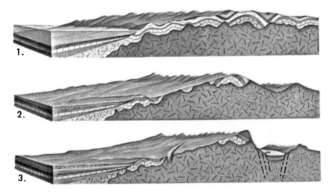

**GEOLOGIC DEVELOPMENT** of Yosemite Valley began many millions of years ago with the birth of the Merced River; but the valley's scenic wonders were not produced until the Sierra was uplifted. From the new height the speed of the river accelerated and cut more

**THE MERCED** at first meandered through a broad valley of low, rolling hills, 500 to 1,000 feet high. Side streams entered the Merced at river level so there were no waterfalls. The climate was warm and the hills forested with broad-leaved trees.

**AN UPLIFT** of the Sierra tilted the land to the west, increasing the Merced's speed and cutting power. Its course through the valley became straighter, and side streams cascaded from hanging valleys (p. 16) as the river cut deeper.

**EARLY GLACIERS** appeared just after the Sierra reached its present height; the Merced was still cutting a narrow, V-shaped gorge about a half mile deep. The climate grew colder and vegetation changed too; conifers replaced the broad-leaved trees.

rapidly. Later, glaciers flowed to polish and sculpt the valley. In parts of Yosemite Valley these powerful forces cut more than a mile deep into the granite block of the Sierra Nevada. Stages in the formation of Yosemite Valley are shown below.

**GLACIERS**, as rivers of ice, moved slowly through Yosemite Valley, grinding and polishing the rocks over which they rode. At Glacier Point the ice was more than 700 ft. thick. Sentinel Dome, Half Dome, El Capitan, and Eagle Peak protruded above.

**ANCIENT LAKE YOSEMITE** was formed when the last glacier cut through the resistant mass of granite and stopped near Bridalveil Fall. The glacier's terminal debris formed a dam that held back the water, issuing from melted snow, to form a lake.

**POSTGLACIAL STREAMS** deposited debris (silt, sand and rocks) and gradually filled Ancient Lake Yosemite. Eventually the lake was reduced to a marsh, later to become the level floor of Yosemite Valley. Polished granite walls loom overhead.

**Exfoliation along Tioga Road**

**Basket Dome with Royal Arches**

**Sentinel Dome**

**North Dome**

**EXFOLIATION,** a process of successive flaking and peeling off of scales of granite, has left behind the arches and domes of Yosemite Park—remnants of Yosemite's ancient landscape. Curved shells, arranged concentrically like layers on an onion, in time break loose and drop off. The outer shells may vary in thickness from 6 inches to several feet. As overlying layers are changed by exposure to air and water, further exfoliation occurs.

**ARCHES,** recessed within one another, are a rare form of rock sculpture produced by exfoliating granite. Royal Arches are an excellent example on a colossal scale. The main arch rises to a height of 1,000 ft. and has a span of 1,800 ft. The layers beneath it range from 10 to 80 feet in thickness. Several unite near the top to form one shell almost 200 ft. thick.

**DOMES** are the highly resistant remains of the ancestral Sierra. Half Dome (p. 4), best known and highest of the Yosemite domes, rises 5,000 feet above the floor of the valley. Ringing the valley's rim are North, Basket and Sentinel domes. From Sentinel Dome one can look down on Yosemite Falls and have a 360-degree panoramic view.

Lembert Dome (top p. 15), one of best known domes in the Tuolumne Meadows, was formed by glaciation rather than exfoliation; has a magnificent view from its top.

**GLACIATION,** in years past, pushed through and gouged out the sides of Yosemite Valley. Evidence that glaciers moved down the mountain and through the valleys is seen on all sides in the upper parts of the park. Along the Tioga Road, rock surfaces shine as if wet, polished to mirror brightness by the abrasives in the glacial ice.

Lembert Dome

**GLACIAL ERRATICS,** rocks of all sizes and shapes, were deposited as glaciers receded. Nowhere is the variety in rocks more apparent than where glaciers rode over domes, as in Tuolumne Meadows and along the Tioga Road. Some erratics formed pedestals—perched erratics—by roofing and protecting softer bedrock that wore away around them. Erratics indicate many things to geologists. Often, this glacial debris is all that remains to show the boundary of an ancient glacier.

Erratics in Tuolumne Meadows

**TERMINAL MORAINES,** piles of debris, are deposited where glaciers end. Lateral moraines were deposited to the sides of glaciers, medial moraines in the middle. One of the most prominent of the several moraines in Yosemite Valley is the Bridalveil Moraine through which a road has been cut near Bridalveil Fall. This terminal moraine dammed Yosemite Valley and formed Ancient Lake Yosemite.

Bridalveil Moraine

Glacially eroded sheepsback, or roche moutonnée, in background in Tuolumne Meadows

**WATERFALLS** of Yosemite are at their fullest in spring and early summer when fed by the melting snows of the High Sierra. Nowhere in the world are there so many spectacular waterfalls concentrated in such a small area as in Yosemite Valley. Many fall free for hundreds of feet. Others are cataracts, tumbling and cascading down the steep valley walls. Except for Vernal, Nevada and Bridalveil, the major waterfalls usually run dry by late summer, then form again with the first rains.

Prior to uplift of Sierra Nevada streams were on the same level.

As the river cut faster, side streams made gulches to it.

After the ice age waterfalls fell from hanging valleys.

**FREE-LEAPING FALLS,** Yosemite, Bridalveil and Ribbon, drop from "hanging valleys" formed when lateral tributaries could not keep pace with the rapid cutting of the Merced River and the grinding force of glaciers.

**THE MERCED RIVER,** pouring over the Giant Stairway (p. 4), forms the Vernal and Nevada Falls where great blocks of granite were quarried and carried away by glaciers. The giant steps are at the east end of the valley.

**CASCADES** such as Sentinel, Royal Arch Cascade and spectacular Staircase Falls splash in successive rock "steps" down the sloping sides of the valley wall. Their waters are considerably diminished by mid-season.

**YOSEMITE'S WATERFALLS** change with the seasons. Many are fed by the waters from melting snows, but a summer thundershower may bring forth hundreds of falls to leap from valley walls, live briefly and disappear.

**YOSEMITE FALLS** (2,425 feet) Yosemite's fame began to spread after this drawing by Thomas A. Ayres was published in 1855. The upper fall is 1,430 feet then a cascade of 675 feet to a final drop of 320 feet, totaling 2,425 feet, the highest water fall in North America.

**VERNAL FALL** (317 ft.), named because mist at its base keeps plants green, is in the Merced River Canyon above Yosemite Valley. Mist Trail leads along the river to top of Vernal Fall.

**NEVADA FALL** (594 ft.) plunges through a narrow chute in contrast to the broad, even lip over which Vernal drops. On Glacier Point Road is an excellent vista of these falls.

**WATERWHEEL FALLS,** about three miles below Glen Aulin, are cascades formed as the Tuolumne River rushes down a steep rock apron. Spumes of water rise and arc back, forming wheel-like shapes.

**BRIDALVEIL FALL** (620 ft.), often the first seen by visitors, is a beautiful free-leaping waterfall. Its wind-blown mists turn rainbow colors. *Pohono*, its Indian name, means "puffing wind." It is one of the more spectacular.

Winter in Yosemite Valley

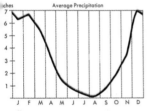

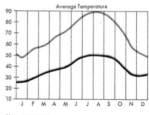

Max. ———
Min. ———

**CLIMATE AND WEATHER.** Despite warm summer days, with the temperature rarely to 100 degrees in Yosemite Valley, the evenings are cool, especially in the high country. Most precipitation occurs in winter, but afternoon thundershowers are common in summer. For hikers, light plastic raincoats or ponchos are a good investment. The first snow usually falls after November 15, the last before April 15. Total winter snow depth averages 74 in. in Yosemite Valley but seldom more than 2 ft. at a time. Snowplows keep the roads open, but tire chains should always be carried.

**THE INDIANS** of Yosemite called themselves Awanee-chees—"the people of the deep, grassy valley." They lived in Yosemite Valley in summer. When winter storms came, most of them moved to the lower, warmer foot-hills. They belonged to the Miwoks, one of the largest Indian tribes on the western slope of the Sierra.

The Awaneechees ate acorns and many kinds of seeds, berries, bulbs and roots. From the streams they caught fish; in the forest were deer, bear and squirrels for meat and fur. Early investigators found about 30 of their "rancherias," or campsites that had been used at various times by Indians in Yosemite Valley. Some of these old camps can be identified today by the obsidian flakes (black, glassy volcanic rock used for arrowheads) and by grinding holes pounded in the bedrock by the women making acorn meal.

**CLOTHING AND SHELTER** were no problem for the Indians in Yosemite's warm summers. The women wore a wrap-around skirt; the men, a simple loin cloth. Both garments were made of tanned deerskin. The children didn't bother with either. Robes, also of animal furs, provided warmth in cooler weather.

For shelter the Indians built teepee-like *uma-chas*. These consisted of poles on which long strips of bark from the Incense-cedars were laid, overlapping so they shed the occasional summer showers. A hole at the peak let out the smoke from small warming fires.

**BASKETS** woven by Yosemite Indian women were used for many purposes. The material used and the method of weaving determined the usefulness of the basket. Some were used to store seeds and other foods; others for carrying heavy burdens or a papoose.

**SHORT BOWS** were made of Incense-cedar; the arrows tipped with points of obsidian traded with Paiute—the neighbors to the East. Obsidian was used also to make skinning knives and other tools. Sharp punches and awls for making baskets and clothing were made from bone.

A successful hunter returns to his village. Deer were an important food for the Awaneechees; animals were hunted also for their furs.

The Indians of Yosemite had many ceremonial dances.

Baskets, skillfully woven, were used in cooking acorn meal.

Currier and Ives lithographed the above Yosemite scene showing Bridalveil Fall. It was hung in many American parlors.

**DISCOVERY OF YOSEMITE** came about when a wounded Grizzly Bear led William Abrams to a spot overlooking the valley. This was in 1849, during the California Gold Rush, which reached as far as the Yosemite foothills. In his diary Abrams described Bridalveil Fall, Cathedral Rocks and Half Dome . . . "a rounded mountain—the valley side of which looked as though it had been sliced with a knife as one would slice a loaf of bread." While Abrams is usually given credit, some historians believe that it was Joseph Walker, during his 1833 expedition (p. 52), who was the first white man to see Yosemite Valley.

In 1851, the Mariposa Battalion, organized under the authority of Governor McDougal, rode into Yosemite Valley in pursuit of Indians who had raided mining camps in the foothills, and rediscovered the Valley's beauty. Its name is based on the Indian name for Grizzly Bear.

**TOURISTS** to Yosemite first arrived in 1855. They were a party of four or five led by James Hutchings, an Englishman gathering material for his *California Magazine*. Yosemite was so little known that they had trouble finding two Indian guides to lead them in. Thomas Ayres, a young artist with Hutchings, made pencil sketches that became the first Yosemite scenes to be published. Word spread rapidly about the beautiful valley in the California mountains. In 1859, Horace Greeley said, "I know of no single wonder of nature on earth which can claim a superiority over the Yosemite."

Getting to Yosemite in those days involved many hardships. From San Francisco, in the early 1870's, a Yosemite-bound traveler would take a river steamer to Stockton, then a stagecoach or mudwagon over poor roads. One 1870 visitor said that a fence six feet from the stagecoach was invisible behind the dust cloud. Finally, a horseback ride led the travelers down steep trails into the Valley. But most agreed that the trip was worth the effort.

**VISITORS** required food and shelter, and so hotels soon began to spring up in Yosemite Valley and along the way. Some were of handhewn timbers, others were roofed with canvas. The first room partitions in the famous Cedar Cottage were made of cheesecloth. Once discovered, it was not long before Yosemite was attracting permanent settlers and with them came a threat that private homesteads would exclude sightseeing visitors from Yosemite Valley.

In the early days, a stagecoach trip to the valley was a slow, rough and dusty ride on the famous Zig Zags, Big Oak Flat Road.

**THE PARK** began as an idea in 1864 when several people who loved Yosemite asked Senator John Conness to request Congress to set aside Yosemite Valley and the Mariposa Grove of Giant Sequoias for the enjoyment of the people, to be held in trust for them. Abraham Lincoln approved the Yosemite Grant, to be kept "inalienable for all time," creating the first State Park in this country. In 1872 Yellowstone was authorized as America's first National Park. Yosemite became a National Park in 1890. State-administered lands in the Park area were ceded to the Federal government in 1905. Yosemite thus became a foundation stone for parks throughout the world.

**NATIONAL PARKS,** such as Yosemite, were first guarded by cavalry soldiers. They chased out poachers and kept the cattle and sheepmen from grazing their animals in the Park. They also mapped the area, laid out many of the trails used today, and stocked fish in the high mountain lakes. Many lakes, streams and passes in Yosemite bear names of cavalrymen.

Troop F of the 6th Cavalry lined up on the Fallen Monarch in the Mariposa Grove in 1899. Yosemite was guarded by U.S. Army cavalrymen from 1891 to 1914.

Ranger naturalists lead nature walks daily in summer.

**THE NATIONAL PARK SERVICE,** established in 1916, took control of the park and rangers. The cavalrymen rode off to the Mexican border raids and to World War I. Thus a colorful era ended and an equally colorful one began.

On back-country patrols, rangers still ride horses as did the early cavalrymen guards, or ski, but much of their travel today is by pickup truck or, in emergencies, by helicopter or Snowcat. These men in stiff-brimmed Stetsons are skilled in many fields. They protect the park and also provide many services for visitors, guarding their safety and making their visits to the park more meaningful by nature walks, museum talks and campfire programs. Behind the scenes are engineers and technicians, administrative and clerical workers, concession operators and others who make the park a pleasant place to visit.

Rangers' duties include helping young visitors find their camps.

Rangers ride horses when patrolling the High Sierra.

The name Yosemite probably came from an Indian word *u-zu-mati* which means Grizzly Bear. Once common in California and featured on the state emblem, the California grizzly is now extinct.

## ANIMALS OF YOSEMITE

A glimpse of a deer or a bear is a highlight for many Yosemite visitors. Some animals, such as the Steller's Jay and the Mule Deer, are common and may be seen almost anytime in Yosemite Valley. Others, like the Mount Lyell Salamander, are rare and hard to find. Because Yosemite has so much variation in elevation— from 2,850 ft. at Arch Rock to 13,114 ft. at Mount Lyell's summit—animals of widely different habitats can live there.

Some of the animals described here are also found in other parts of North America. They are included because they are often seen by visitors to the park.

**MAMMALS** in Yosemite range in size from large Mule Deer and Mountain Lions to tiny shrews, the smallest and most voracious of mammals. About 80 species of mammals have been recorded. Wood rats, Ringtail Cats and others active at night are seldom seen by visitors. But many are active during the day, and everywhere—from the flat country of Yosemite Valley to the rocky high country—you will see them if you look closely enough.

**MULE DEER** are abundant in the Park and tend to lose their shyness in Yosemite Valley where they are exposed constantly to people. They are often seen browsing on twigs and leaves. Despite their gentle appearance, deer can be dangerous, particularly mothers protecting their young. Enjoy them from a safe distance and never feed them.

The bucks, or males, shed their antlers and grow new ones every year. The antlers are used in fighting for mates during the mating season. Bucks stand about 3.5 ft. tall at the shoulder and may weigh over 200 lbs. Does, or females, are smaller. Fawns, born in early summer, usually retain their white spots until winter, then become gray.

**BIGHORN SHEEP** (3 ft. tall at shoulder, 200 lbs.), now rare in Yosemite, were once common along the crest of the Sierra. They were hunted for food and many died from diseases caught from domestic sheep. Lone individuals are seen occasionally. It is hoped that these mountain-dwellers can be reestablished. Both rams and ewes have horns.

**BLACK BEARS** (5 ft.) may be brown, cinnamon or black—all color phases of the same animal. Tiny when born, bears may grow to more than 500 lbs. Bears will eat almost anything—fish, small rodents, and berries in the wild, cookies or other provisions at your camp. They will normally avoid people unless attracted by food. Do not feed them!

**RACCOON** (32 in.) is easily recognized by its black mask and ringed tail. Active at night, it walks flat-footed, like a bear, and uses its front paws like hands. Eats fruits and berries, insects and other small animals, often dunking them in water before eating. Heavier, shorter-tailed, and less shy than the Ringtail. Common in Yosemite lower country.

**RINGTAIL** (28 in.) has a slender body and no mask. A good climber, it frequents trees and rocky slopes. The catlike Ringtail feeds on mice and other small animals and may enter buildings at night to hunt for them. During the Gold Rush days, prospectors kept Ringtails in camp to catch mice, earning the animals the name Miner's Cats.

**BOBCAT** or Wildcat (30 in.), has a short tail and soft, thick spotted fur. It can climb trees but often makes its den in rocky places. Though wary, Bobcats are sometimes seen in the meadows in early evening hunting for mice and birds. Not common in Yosemite Valley.

**MOUNTAIN LION** (6 ft.) helps keep the deer herds from becoming too numerous for their food supply, a sometimes critical problem in Yosemite. Seldom seen, the largest of the North American cats is brown on top and light on the underside, with black on the tip of its long, graceful tail. Kittens, 2 or 3, are spotted.

OF VALLEYS AND FOOTHILLS 29

**Red Fox**

**Gray Fox**

**Spotted Skunk**

**Striped Skunk**

**COYOTES** (45 in.) are common in Yosemite but are shy and will not normally come near people. Often they are heard howling and barking at night, or they may be seen trotting across meadows or along the roads as they hunt for mice, their main food. Yosemite's mountain coyote has long, grayish fur, lighter on underside, darkish tail.

**FOXES,** both the Red and the Gray, are graceful and almost catlike. The Red Fox, rare in Yosemite, has black legs and a white tip on its tail. The Gray Fox, common in the Park, has gray legs and varying amounts of yellowish-red fur. Its tail is black-tipped, with a black stripe along the top.

**SKUNKS,** most common in the foothills, are nocturnal. Their diet consists of insects, rodents, lizards, an occasional bird and some plant food. They use their long claws for digging. When a skunk lifts its plumelike tail, it is ready to spray its potent musk. The scent is discharged only when the skunk is frightened or attacked. Keep your distance.

The Spotted Skunk (15 in.) stands on its forefeet when threatened. The Striped Skunk (24 in.) forages for food at dusk without fear of man or animals. The white stripe running down its back from head to tail varies in width with individuals. Despite bad reputations, skunks are important animals.

**LONG-TAILED WEASEL (14 in.)** is light brown above and yellow-orange underneath in summer. The Ermine, or Short-tailed Weasel (8 in.), is darker brown above, lighter below. Both usually turn white in winter except for the black tip of their tail. Extremely swift, weasels prey on mice, rats and other animals.

**BADGER (30 in.)** is grizzled brown-gray, squat, and powerful, with sturdy legs. It uses its long, heavy front claws to dig out squirrels or other burrowers or to escape a pursuer. If cornered, it may emit a strong scent.

**PORCUPINES (36 in.)** are easily identified by their long, sharp quills. When in danger, porcupines roll into a ball. They strike with their tail but cannot "throw" their quills. They feed mainly on the buds and bark of trees.

**BEAVER (40 in.),** largest U.S. rodent, has a flat, scaly tail and webbed hind feet. It cuts trees for food (the twigs and bark) and for building dams. The dams may be useful in controlling erosion, or harmful, depending on what is flooded. Beavers were introduced into the park near Wawona and Glen Aulin.

Long-tailed Weasel

Short-tailed Weasel

**WESTERN GRAY SQUIRREL (12 in.)** has a long, bushy tail that serves as a balance when the squirrel moves among the tree-tops. Gray above, with slight pepper and salt effect; under-parts white. Once rare, now fairly common in the Park.

**DOUGLAS' SQUIRREL,** or Sierra Chickaree (10 in.), lives in trees and always seems to be in a hurry. The Chickaree scolds in-truders with shrill, birdlike tones. Its food is mainly pine seeds. Steel gray and brownish above, underparts buff to white.

**NORTHERN FLYING SQUIRREL (10 in.),** common but seldom seen because it is active at night, is gray on top, white below. It glides from top of one tree to bottom of another, using the thin skin between its legs as a glider, its flat tail to steer.

**CALIFORNIA GROUND SQUIRREL (15 in.)** lives in burrows. It is brown, speckled with white. The white mantle across its shoulder distinguishes it. May become dormant twice a year—during the cold of winter and in sum-mer when it is hot and dry.

**POCKET GOPHERS** (6 in.) live in burrows, the entrance marked by mounds of loose dirt. Fur-lined pockets on each side of the Pocket Gopher's sharp, chisel-like front teeth are used for carrying seeds and other plant food to be stored.

**CHIPMUNKS** (6-8 in.) are reddish brown with four light-colored stripes separated by dark on the back. Stripes on the head run to the tip of the nose. Five kinds of chipmunks live in Yosemite, and they may be seen at most elevations.

**DUSKY-FOOTED WOOD RAT**, or Pack Rat (15 in.), may steal bright objects from a cabin and pack them off to its stick nest. In exchange it may leave a seed, pebble or whatever it is carrying. Common in foothills but nocturnal, hence rarely seen.

**WHITE-FOOTED MICE** (6 in.) are warm brown above, with a pure white belly and feet. These agile, long-tailed rodents are active at night. Four species live in Yosemite. They are prevalent everywhere except on the snow-capped peaks. Two most common of the white-footed mice are Deer and Brush Mice.

**MEADOW MICE**, or Voles (6 in.), are chunky grass-eating rodents, with short tails, short ears, and thick, dark-brown fur. Their runways thread through the tangled grasses of meadows. Meadow mice are active all year, even beneath the snow. They are food of predatory birds and mammals.

Deer Mouse

California Meadow Mouse

Brush Mouse

Mountain Meadow Mouse

**GOLDEN-MANTLED GROUND SQUIRREL** (10 in.) is often mistaken for a chipmunk, but the broad white stripes on its back run only to its shoulders. Lives higher in the mountains than the California Ground Squirrel. Common around Glacier Point.

**BELDING GROUND SQUIRREL** (10 in.) is often called Picket Pin because it sits so erect it looks like a stake driven into the ground. Small, usually tan, it lives mainly on grass and plant foods. Has high, shrill, chattering voice; hibernates in winter.

**CONY,** or Pika (6 in.), has a short face and rounded ears, like a Guinea Pig. Closely related to the rabbits, it lives in the rock piles in the high country. The Cony does not hibernate and survives the winter by feeding on grasses and other plants, which are harvested, dried and stored in piles beneath rock overhangs during summer and fall. Often a Cony can be heard chirping or bleating from its rock perch.

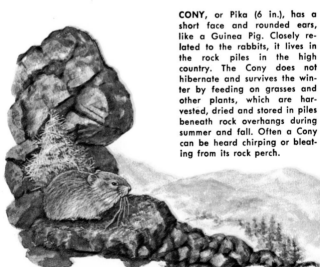

**YELLOW-BELLIED MARMOT (24 in.)**, largest of the squirrel family, resembles the eastern Woodchuck. It lives in the High Sierra and enjoys sunning on warm rocks when not feeding or sleeping. If danger threatens, the Marmot whistles shrilly.

**FISHER (36 in.)**, now rare, has dark brown fur, gray on neck and shoulders and often with white on breast. The Fisher is an agile climber, living in high forests. Its food is mainly small rodents, but it has been known to kill porcupines.

**MARTEN (24 in.)**, also called American Sable, is a rich brown above, with orange or buff on its throat. The Marten lives in forests and among rock slides in the high country; is seldom seen. It is as agile as a cat in climbing.

**WOLVERINE (36 in.)** is Yosemite's rarest furbearer, and little is known about its life in the Park. Stockily built, it has a bearlike head, thick forelegs and a bushy tail. This animal lives in the High Sierra, close to timberline.

**BIRDS** of more than 200 species may be seen and enjoyed in Yosemite. If you camp, your table is almost certain to be visited by the noisy, brilliant blue Steller's Jay and the cheerful Black-headed Grosbeak as they help themselves to your food. The silence of the night will be interrupted by the hooting of owls.

**GOLDEN EAGLE** (32 in.), largest land bird of the Sierra, may have a wingspan of more than 6 ft. Dark brown, with some white at base of tail. Immatures have more white. Often seen soaring over the cliffs.

**RED-TAILED HAWK** (18 in.) is seen in Yosemite at all elevations. It likes to perch on high, dead snags. Identified in flight by the brick-red underside of its tail. The top of the tail is a bright rust-red. Dark brown body; streaked with white.

**OSPREY**, or Fish Hawk (22 in.), lives near water. It perches or hovers until a fish is sighted, then plunges into the water feet first. May be seen at Hetch Hetchy or on one of the large lakes.

**KESTREL** (11 in.), sometimes miscalled Sparrow Hawk, feeds mainly on small rodents and insects. Rust-red tail and back, and narrow, pointed wings. It often perches on power lines.

Serious bird watching requires a degree of patience, a bird guide and binoculars. Go a short distance from the traveled path to look for birds and listen to their songs and calls. Sitting quietly and letting the birds come by is often better than going in search of them. Most species are common in other parts of the country.

**GREAT HORNED OWL** (20 in.) is more often heard than seen. From dusk to dawn, its deep voice sounds through the forests. A large brown, gray and white owl, its "horns" are feathered ear tufts, which it can raise.

**GREAT GRAY OWL** (22 in.), mottled gray with white streaks, is the largest of the Yosemite owls and, because it is rare, the most sought by bird watchers. It is unafraid of people. Seen most often at an elevation of 6,000 to 7,000 ft.

**SCREECH OWL** (8 in.) has conspicuous ear tufts. A widespread American bird, this small, gray-and-black-streaked owl often lives in oak trees and nests in holes in trees. Its call is a series of tremulous whistles.

**PYGMY OWL** (6 in.), smallest of the Yosemite owls, is active during the day. Its voice is a single "toot" or a slow series on the same note. The Pygmy Owl lacks ear tufts and has a long tail. Note black on back of its neck.

**CALIFORNIA QUAIL** (8 in.) are birds of brush and grasslands. Sometimes flocks are seen running along the road. When frightened, they flush with a loud whirring of wings, on a brief flight. The head plume is short and bends forward, distinguishing it from the Mountain Quail found on p. 45. This is California's state bird.

**BAND-TAILED PIGEON** (13.5 in) lives and feeds in flocks. In size and shape it resembles the domestic pigeon. Note the white neck band, yellow bill and grey tail with black band. Sometimes flocks perch in tall trees and sun on bare branches. The Band-tailed Pigeon is common in Yosemite Valley and can be seen at any time of year.

**SPOTTED SANDPIPER** (6.5 in.) constantly bobs its tail and teeters as it walks along shores hunting for small animals. Call is a clear whistle uttered two or three times in succession. Bill is long (to 1 in.) in proportion to the bird's sizes. Breast is spotted in summer, clear in winter.

**DIPPER** or Water Ouzel (6 in.), bobs up and down as it stands or walks along mountain streams. It holds its short tail at a jaunty angle and actually walks underwater in the cascades to pick up insect larvae and nymphs. Its feathers shed water; feet are not webbed.

**BLACK PHOEBE** (6 in.), a flycatcher, commonly perches on limbs along Sierran streams. It darts out after insects, then returns to the same perch where it sits with its tail wagging. Note the black on its head and shoulders and white underparts. Nests under bridges, or on the sides of cliffs or buildings.

**WESTERN WOOD PEWEE** (5 in.) is a common flycatcher in both broad-leaved and conifer forests of Yosemite. Often seen perched on low branches, from which it darts out to catch insects. Inconspicuously marked, it has a quiet, descending call which it repeats frequently. Commonly sings continuously.

**OLIVE-SIDED FLYCATCHER** (6 in.) has a three-noted call that is unforgettable. The second note is much higher than the first or third, as though saying, "What peeves you?" Usually seen perched on the limbs of dead trees. Bill is larger and tail shorter than Wood Pewee's.

**BELTED KINGFISHER** (12. in.) announces its coming with a rattling call. It flies over streams and lakes looking for fish, which it catches by plunging into the water headfirst. Has a large crest and heavy bill; blue on back and in a band across white breast. The female has two breast bands-one blue, the other tan. Common in the U.S.

**PILEATED WOODPECKER** (15 in.) has been called Cock of the Woods because of its large size. When digging for food, its bill pounds like a hammer; chips are thrown several feet. Flies in a direct course with slow wingbeats. Has a red crest. Call is a loud "kuk." Found widely in the U.S. but is a rare sight today in Yosemite's coniferous forests.

**ACORN WOODPECKER** (8 in.) is common in Yosemite Valley and most abundant in oak trees. It drills holes in trees, fenceposts, and buildings and often stores acorns in them for future use. Usually seen in groups of two or three.

**RED-SHAFTED FLICKER** (11 in.) is a handsome woodpecker with a noisy call note. White rump patch shows in flight, as does light red under wings and tail. Unlike most woodpeckers, it feeds on the ground, eating ants and other insects. Flight is undulating.

**ALLEN'S HUMMINGBIRD** (3 in.) is smaller than Anna's. Rare, it has a copper-red throat and chin bordered with white. Both sexes have bronze-green backs and cinnamon-brown tails.

**ANNA'S HUMMINGBIRD** (3.5 in.) is best-known and largest hummingbird in Yosemite. Head and throat iridescent red in male; both sexes have metallic green backs. Common in foothills.

**VIOLET-GREEN SWALLOW** (5 in.) has white on its underside; its back and head are an iridescent green. There is a violet tinge on its rump, just behind two distinctive white patches. Nests in cavities in trees or crevices on cliffs. The Violet-green Swallow flies high when feeding. This is the most common swallow seen in the Yosemite Valley.

**CLIFF SWALLOW** (5 in.), famous for its returns to Mission Capistrano, builds mud nests on buildings or cliffs. Wings, tail and back are black; black patch on throat. Rump brown, forehead white. Feeds on insects as it skims over water.

**WHITE-THROATED SWIFT** (6.5 in.) may whiz by your head like an arrow if you are at Glacier Point or Sentinel Dome. Black with white flanks and breast. Nests and roosts in crevices in the rock cliffs. This swift is swallow-like, but wings are longer and slimmer.

**YELLOW-RUMPED WARBLER** (5 in.) is black, white and gray, with yellow on shoulders, throat and rump. Common in conifer forests in summer, in broad-leaved trees in autumn, spring.

**KINGLETS** move in small flocks in treetops. Calls faint, high-pitched. Ruby-crowned Kinglet (4 in.), crown often obscure, travels alone. Golden-crowned (3.5 in.) has bright crown.

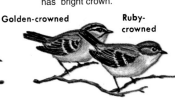

Golden-crowned          Ruby-crowned

**STELLER'S JAY** (11 in.) is bright blue with a prominent crest. In addition to its raucous, scolding call, it has a pleasant song that is warbled softly. Steller's Jay spends much of its time in trees and often visits campsites and picnic tables in search of food.

**BREWER'S BLACKBIRD** (8 in.) travels in flocks. Males are shiny black with a hint of purple and with white eyes. Females are drab brown with dark eyes. Foraging on lawns and meadows, clucking as they walk, they feed on worms and insects.

**RED-WINGED BLACKBIRD** (7.5 in.) nests in marshes and wet meadows in Yosemite Valley. In courting, the shiny, black male lifts red epaulets and fluffs his feathers. His wings droop, and he spreads his tail feathers. Females are dark brown with streaks on breast.

**BROWN-HEADED COWBIRD** (6.5 in.) resembles a small blackbird, with dark eyes. Often lifts head and points bill skyward. Male has a brown head and shoulders. Female, all brown, lays eggs in nest of a "foster" parent, which raises her young.

**PINE SISKIN** (4.5 in.) is a small bird with brown-and-white-streaked plumage. Middle of wing and base of tail yellow; tail deeply notched. Often seen in flocks. Flight undulating.

**CANYON WREN** (4.5 in.) has a melodious song of 10 or more clear trills, starting high and falling rapidly. Rich brown with a white throat. Hops in zigzag path, bobbing often. Keeps tail tilted upward.

**WHITE-CROWNED SPARROW** (6 in.) has three white stirpes on its head. Upper body streaked gray-brown, light gray beneath. This jaunty sparrow feeds in the grasslands but stays close to thickets that provide perches, nesting sites and escape from enemies.

**WESTERN TANAGERS** (6.5 in.) are beautiful birds-the males black, white and yellow with a red head; the females greenish yellow. Not shy, they sometimes come to picnic tables for food. In spring and early summer, main food is insects; later in year, seeds and berries.

**JUNCO** (5.5 in.) is common in summer and autumn. It flicks its white outer tail feathers constantly. Male's head and breast black; light gray in female. Both are light brown on back. Feeds in flocks.

**RED-BREASTED NUTHATCH** (4 in.) is often heard before seen. Its call is a nasal "yank." Tail short, squared. Probes bark for insects. Note white eye stripe. Common in Yosemite Valley.

**BROWN CREEPER** (5 in.) creeps on tree bark, moving upward in a spiral, probing for insects. Uses tail feathers as a brace. Bill slender, curved. Call a high, tinny lisp.

**TOWNSEND'S SOLITAIRE** (9 in.) has a melodic, robin-like song, heard all year long. Tail white on the edges; has a white eye ring. Catches insects on the wing like a flycatcher. Common in Red-fir forests in summer; in Yosemite Valley in winter. Nests on ground.

**VARIED THRUSH** (8 in.) is a handsome, robin-like bird with a black "bib" across its orange-brown breast and a stripe of orange behind the eye and on the wings. Upperparts uniformly gray. Found mainly in woodlands. Sometimes called Alaska Robin.

**BLACK-HEADED GROSBEAK** (7.5 in.) has heavy, seed-eating bill and conspicuous black, white, and orange markings. In summer Yosemite Valley resounds with its warbling, robin-like song. Sociable, it will take food from picnic tables and camps.

**WESTERN BLUEBIRD** (5.5 in.) is bright blue above, rusty-red beneath. Prefers the foothills but occasionally seen in the high country. In spring and early summer, pairs are seen hunting insects near grasslands. A favorite food is mistletoe berries.

**BLUE OR DUSKY GROUSE (17 in.)** are chicken-like, dark-gray birds. Males have an orange or yellow eye patch. Males' drum-like booming can be heard during the mating season. Nest on ground; are unafraid and will allow people to approach.

**CLARK'S NUTCRACKER (11 in.)**, light gray with a white face and black-and-white wings, is seen most often in conifers near the timberline. Voice is a repeated crowlike "caw." Feeds on pine seeds. Sometimes it takes tidbits from tables at campsites.

**MOUNTAIN BLUEBIRD (6 in.)** is all blue and a bit larger than the rusty-breasted Western Bluebird. Summers in the High Sierra. Often hovers while it searches below for insects. Nests in tree cavities in the Lodgepole Pine belt. Winters in foothills.

**GRAY-CROWNED ROSY FINCH (6 in.)** is most often seen by mountaineers in the High Sierra above timberline, where it nests. Flies in flocks to glaciers and snowfields; feeds on seeds and insects. Unafraid of people.

**MOUNTAIN QUAIL, (9 in.)** is a handsome bird with a slim, erect head plume that distinguishes it from the California Quail. The Mountain Quail prefers brush and forests to 7,000 ft. or higher, but is sometimes seen at lower elevations.

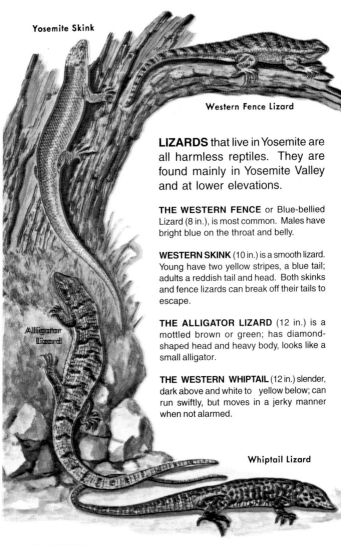

Yosemite Skink

Western Fence Lizard

Alligator Lizard

Whiptail Lizard

**LIZARDS** that live in Yosemite are all harmless reptiles. They are found mainly in Yosemite Valley and at lower elevations.

**THE WESTERN FENCE** or Blue-bellied Lizard (8 in.), is most common. Males have bright blue on the throat and belly.

**WESTERN SKINK** (10 in.) is a smooth lizard. Young have two yellow stripes, a blue tail; adults a reddish tail and head. Both skinks and fence lizards can break off their tails to escape.

**THE ALLIGATOR LIZARD** (12 in.) is a mottled brown or green; has diamond-shaped head and heavy body, looks like a small alligator.

**THE WESTERN WHIPTAIL** (12 in.) slender, dark above and white to yellow below; can run swiftly, but moves in a jerky manner when not alarmed.

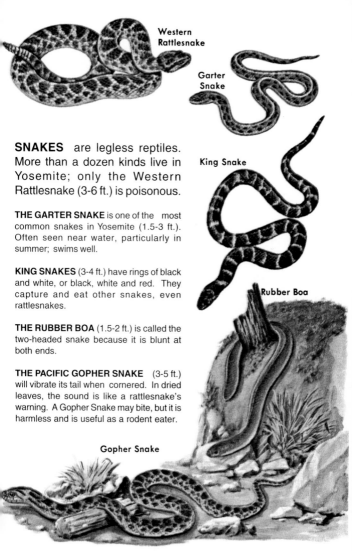

**Western Rattlesnake**

**Garter Snake**

**King Snake**

**Rubber Boa**

**SNAKES** are legless reptiles. More than a dozen kinds live in Yosemite; only the Western Rattlesnake (3-6 ft.) is poisonous.

**THE GARTER SNAKE** is one of the most common snakes in Yosemite (1.5-3 ft.). Often seen near water, particularly in summer; swims well.

**KING SNAKES** (3-4 ft.) have rings of black and white, or black, white and red. They capture and eat other snakes, even rattlesnakes.

**THE RUBBER BOA** (1.5-2 ft.) is called the two-headed snake because it is blunt at both ends.

**THE PACIFIC GOPHER SNAKE** (3-5 ft.) will vibrate its tail when cornered. In dried leaves, the sound is like a rattlesnake's warning. A Gopher Snake may bite, but it is harmless and is useful as a rodent eater.

**Gopher Snake**

California Newt, or Waterdog

Ensatinas, or Sierra Nevada Salamander

## SALAMANDERS AND NEWTS,
amphibians with tails, usually have 4 toes on front feet.

**THE CALIFORNIA NEWT,** or Waterdog (6 in.), is common in the foothills. Upper surface chocolate to dark brown; orange to yellow underneath. Lays eggs in streams and ponds.

**ENSATINAS,** or Sierra Nevada Salamanders (5 in.), have prominent orange spots on their dark brown body; light gray underneath. They lay their eggs in damp places but not in water.

**MOUNT LYELL SALAMANDER** (4 in.) is rare; was first discovered in Yosemite. This small amphibian has a flattened head and body; has broad, flat feet. Dark chocolate color above, lighter on underside. Is found under rocks or in other damp places, even at the top of Half Dome.

Mount Lyell Salamander

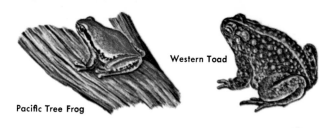
Pacific Tree Frog

Western Toad

## FROGS AND TOADS, amphibians more often heard than seen. Lack tails as adults.

**THE PACIFIC TREEFROG** (2 in.) has a black eye stripe and tiny "suction cups" at the ends of its toes and can climb smooth surfaces.

**THE WESTERN TOAD** (5 in.) is heavy-bodied. It seldom hops but walks, dragging its hind feet.

Yosemite Toad

**THE YOSEMITE TOAD** (3 in.) lives in high country; closely resembles the Western Toad. Active from May to October.

Red-legged Frog

**THE RED-LEGGED FROG** (5 in.) has pinkish-red hind legs and a prominent hump on its back. Is found at lower elevations up to 4,000 ft.

**THE YELLOW-LEGGED FROG** (3 in.) is the most common frog in Yosemite; is dark above and whitish below, with yellow on the undersides of its hind legs.

Yellow-legged Frog

**FISHES** were not abundant in Yosemite waters originally. Of the game fishes in Yosemite, only the Rainbow Trout is native. The glacier-scoured lakes above the high waterfalls had no fish until trout were planted there by early settlers and by the U.S. Cavalry. Now these waters are managed by the National Park Service. Fingerling trout once were dropped from aircraft. The Eastern Brook

**GOLDEN TROUT**, called the world's most beautiful trout, originated in the southern Sierra and has been planted in several streams in Yosemite. Golden-yellow on sides, with reddish on fins; undersurface white, grows to 18 in. long.

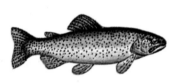

**RAINBOW TROUT** has tiny black spots on its sides and a full-length red to violet band. The only native Yosemite trout, formerly limited to river systems below waterfalls but now in many high lakes. Rainbows most often caught run from 6 to 8 in.

**BROOK TROUT** are fish taken most often in the park's high mountain streams and lakes. The Brook Trout's back is a mottled olive-green, and the spots on its sides vary from gray to red. Leading edges of lower fins are usually white. Grows to over 20 in.

**BROWN TROUT**, also called Loch Leven, has red and black spots on its sides. This European trout is found in the Merced River and similar streams in the Sierra. One caught in Yosemite weighed 12 lbs. and was 27 in. long. Most are from 8 to 10 in. long.

Trout and the Brown Trout adapted best. Today, there are five non-game species that are native to Yosemite's streams, particularly in the Merced and Tuolumne rivers. Natural distribution of fish in Yosemite National Park is very limited. A California fishing license is required to fish in the park. Check at any ranger station for current regulations.

**SUCKERS** feed along the bottom, using their "vacuum cleaner" thick-lipped mouth to draw in organic matter. Length to 24 in.; color, green brown. Native to rivers below waterfalls. Introduced to Tenaya Lake.

**CALIFORNIA ROACH**, has large eyes and pointed head, is less than 6 in. long. Found in Hetch Hetchy Reservoir and Merced River. Probably important as food for larger fish.

**RIFFLE SCULPIN** is grotesque, with a large head, mouth and mottled pectoral fins. It is found in the Merced River near and below Park boundary. Less than 6 in. long.

**HARDHEAD** is a minnow but may grow to more than 2 ft. Body slender with a heavy head; color, yellow green. Uncommon in Yosemite, but a few have been caught in Merced River near Park.

**SACRAMENTO SQUAWFISH** are large minnows common in foothill streams of the Sierra. Solid brown or green, with silver on the sides. Large head and mouth and a slender body, up to 3 ft.

Plants in Yosemite range from primitive fungi and lichens to the Giant Sequoias, largest of living things. More than 1,500 kinds of plants grow in the park. Like all natural features, plants are protected in Yosemite National Park. This assures visitors an opportunity to see natural communities of plants and animals in a land rapidly being changed by man.

**CONE-BEARING TREES** (Conifers) of 18 species grow in Yosemite. Each kind is adapted to grow best in a particular environment. Most abundant from 3,000 to 7,000 feet and can be identified easily.

**GIANT SEQUOIAS** are native only to a narrow strip some 250 miles long on the west slope of the Sierra in California. Some grow to heights of more than 300 ft. Yosemite has three groves (see map). Mariposa Grove, largest in Yosemite, contains about 200 giant trees 10 feet or more in diameter and thousands of younger ones. Tuolumne Grove has about 25 giants; Merced, 20.

Zenas Leonard, clerk of the Walker Expedition, wrote in his diary, "In the last two days of traveling we have found some trees of the Redwood species, incredibly large." Historians agree that this was either the Merced Grove or the Tuolumne Grove. This was the first reported discovery of the Giant Sequoia.

One of the first men to explore the Mariposa Grove was Galen Clark, in 1857. Clark was important to Yosemite history as the first Guardian of the Yosemite and Big Trees Grants of 1864. A replica of the cabin he built is now in the Mariposa Grove Museum. When the Coulterville Road was being built into Yosemite Valley in the early 1870's, the survey party laying out its route found the Merced Grove. They rerouted the road so that stagecoach passengers could see the trees.

A tunnel was cut through the Wawona Tree in 1881 to attract visitors to the Mariposa Grove. Today, cutting such a tunnel would be considered vandalism, but it made this tree one of the best known in the world! The Grizzly Giant, largest tree in the Mariposa Grove, is 210 ft. tall and measures 96.5 ft. around at its base. The first limb to branch out from its trunk (at 95 ft.) is 6 ft. in diameter, larger than the trunk diameter of many trees.

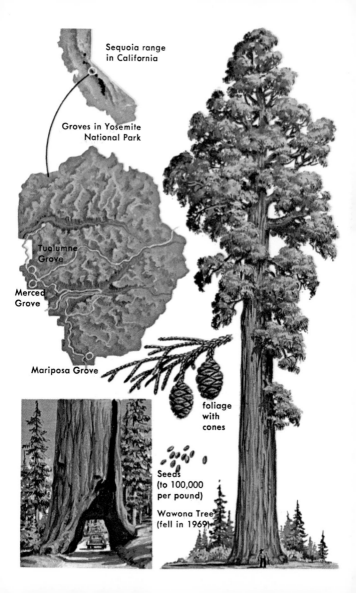

Sequoia range
in California

Groves in Yosemite
National Park

Tuolumne
Grove

Merced
Grove

Mariposa Grove

foliage
with
cones

Seeds
(to 100,000
per pound)

Wawona Tree
(fell in 1969)

The Grizzly Giant

Tree rings reveal age of tree

**THE GRIZZLY GIANT** is estimated to contain 363,500 board feet of lumber, but its brittle wood would have little commercial value. Lumbermen found the Giant Sequoias difficult to handle. Many, felled in the early days, had to be blown apart with dynamite to get pieces small enough to fit wagons and saws. Up to 80 percent of the trees were wasted.

A few Giant Sequoias are cut on privately owned land today, and their wood is made into shakes or stakes for grapevines. Fortunately many are being preserved in national parks and forests and also in state parks.

**THE AGE OF A SEQUOIA** is determined by counting its annual rings. The oldest Sequoia known from such a ring count was 3,200 years old. The age of living trees can only be estimated by comparing their trunk size to the trunks of trees nearby that have been cut. On this basis, some tree experts have calculated the Grizzly Giant to be the oldest of the Giant Sequoias, with an estimated age of more than 2,000 years. Others give this distinction to the General Sherman tree in Sequoia National Park. Only the grotesquely gnarled Bristlecone Pines in the White Mountains east of the Sierra are known, by actual count, to be older. With no enemies other than lightning and man, the ancient Giant Sequoias still living today can conceivably live for countless generations more.

Giant Sequoias in Mariposa Grove

**FIRES** have been of great value for survival of the sequoia species. The fires destroyed competitive plants, and the burned litter on the forest floor created ash-covered seedbeds in which the tiny seeds could sprout and find sunlight.

Many of these large trees bear scars of fires that have swept the groves in centuries past. Because of their thick, noncombustible bark, the trees are fire resistant.

**FIRE PROTECTION** has been so successful as to be a hazard. In many of the groves fire protection has allowed the undergrowth to grow to such a size that a fire today could kill the sequoias. In addition, recent research indicates that sequoias may require fire in order to reproduce. Fire will burn up young trees, but has killed few, if any, of the giants. Experiments are teaching man to use fire rather than allow it to be an enemy.

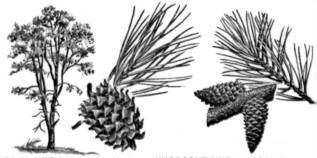

**GRAY PINE** (to 60 ft.) lacks the symmetry of many pines but has a ruggedness that makes it blend into its foothill surroundings. Grayish-green needles, 8 to 10 in. long, are in 3's. Heavy prickly cones are 6 to 12 in. long.

**KNOBCONE PINE** (to 75 ft.), also a foothill species, has cones that open and release seeds only after a fire. The cones are smaller than those of Gray Pine and are in clusters on the main trunk. Needles are in 3's and may be 5 in. long.

**PONDEROSA**, or Yellow Pine, grows to six ft. in diameter, 200 ft. high, and has yellow-orange bark. The scales on the bark fit together like a jigsaw puzzle. Needles in 3's, up to 12 in. long. Cones are small and 5 to 7 in. in length. Common in Yosemite Valley.

**DOUGLAS FIR** (to 125 ft.) has more than 20 common names. One is Bottle-brush Tree because of the way the needles project from all sides of the branches. Small, papery cones have distinctive three-pointed bracts. This tall, rugged tree is common along western Sierra to 7,000 ft.

**WHITE FIR** (to 200 ft.) needles are more greenish than Red Fir's (p.59) and each has a half-twist at its base. Cones are similar but longer. White Fir grows at lower elevations but both can be seen along Glacier Point and Tioga roads.

**TORREYA**, or California Nutmeg (to 50 ft.), has foliage similar to a fir. Needles, to 2 in. long, are flattened and sharp, and blue-green fruit is the size of a large walnut. Common along Merced River above Park's Arch Rock Entrance.

**SINGLELEAF PINYONS** (to 25 ft.) are usually rounded; the stiff, sharp-pointed needles, to 2 in. long, are borne single. Common in arid country on east side of Tioga Pass. Nuts were once an important food of Indians and are eaten by some wildlife.

**INCENSE-CEDAR**, (to 100 ft.) is commonly mistaken for the Giant Sequoia (p52) but has flattened foliage. Bark is reddish brown. Small cones (1 in.) divide into three parts when they open. Common in Yosemite Valley, mixed with other conifers.

**WESTERN WHITE PINE** (to 125 ft.) has needles in 5's, like Sugar Pine, but the cones, hanging at ends of branches, are smaller. Grows from about 7,500 ft. to timberline and is common along the Tioga Road. Also called Silver Pine.

**JEFFREY PINE** (to 175 ft.) resembles Ponderosa Pine but grows at higher elevations, the bark is darker, and cones do not prick the hand when squeezed. Bark smells like vanilla or pineapples. Needles are in 3's and are 5 to 10 in. long. Common at Glacier Point.

**SUGAR PINE** (to 175 ft.), largest and most majestic of pines, produces cones to 24 in. long. Branches curve outward, like extended arms. Needles, in 5's, are up to 3 in. in length. Seen along Wawona and Big Oak Flat roads.

**LODGEPOLE PINE** (to 100 ft.), the only pine in Yosemite with short needles in 2's, has fine-grained, yellowish bark. The cones are not over 3 in. long. Grows tall and slender in dense stands in high country areas. These trees may be dwarfed when growing near timberline.

**WHITEBARK PINE** has needles in 5's. The purple, pitchy cones disintegrate on the tree. Common around Tioga Pass and is characteristic of timberline regions, where it is dwarfed and shrubby. On lower slopes, grows erect, to 35 ft.

**SIERRA JUNIPER** (to 50 ft.) thrives on rocky slopes at high elevations. Tiny, grayish-green scales overlap; small cones are black and berry-like. Bark dark red. Many of the oldest junipers grow along Tioga Road; rival Giant Sequoia in longevity.

**RED FIR** (to 150 ft.), the "Silvertip" of the Christmas tree trade, has bluish needles (blue-green when new). Cones stand up like candles in tops of slender trees. Bark is smooth and white on young trees, dark red, rough and ridged on older trees.

**MOUNTAIN HEMLOCK** (to 100 ft.), another high-country conifer, has needles less than an inch long attached singly to branches that grow completely to the ground. A graceful tree, the Mountain Hemlock is a contrast to the more rugged trees.

**BROAD-LEAVED TREES**, fewer in number than cone-bearing trees, are concentrated in Yosemite Valley. Before shedding their leaves in fall, broad-leaved trees put on a brilliant show of autumn colors. Black Oaks, Aspens and Dogwood are among the most spectacular.

**QUAKING ASPEN'S** leaves shimmer in the slightest breeze. The bark is white and smooth, and the leaves turn yellow or orange in autumn. Common in high, moist places. Grows to 50 ft.

**WHITE ALDER** (to 100 ft.) has smooth, gray bark and dark green leaves with prominent veins and tiny marginal teeth. Found along streamsides up to 7,000 ft., but most common at lower elevations. Flowers in tiny "cones" about half an inch long.

**COTTONWOOD** (to 90 ft.) is a water-loving tree common in foothills and rare above 4,000 ft. Broad leaves are bright green on top and light below, with prominent veins. Bark gray and smooth on young trees; thick, rough and grooved on older trees.

**WILLOWS** (to 25 ft.) usually grow along streams or in other wet places. Some of the more than a dozen species found in the Sierra are shrubby or dwarfed, as in the timberline Alpine Willow (4-6 in. tall). Willows have slender, pointed leaves. The catkins are the flowers.

**BLACK OAK** (to 75 ft.) is the common oak of Yosemite Valley, and its acorns were ground for food by Indians (pp. 20-21). Bark is dark gray to black, and deeply lobed leaves are dark green on top, lighter underneath. In autumn, leaves turn golden brown.

**BLUE OAK** grows among Digger Pines in the dry country of the foothills. Its leaves have a blue-green cast, woolly beneath, and less deeply lobed than those of the Black Oak. Blue Oak grows to a height of about 60 ft. in good soil.

**CANYON LIVE OAK** (to 75 ft.) is an evergreen. Its leaves are green above, dusty-yellow beneath. Leaf margins usually smooth on old trees but commonly notched, like holly, in young trees. Sometimes called Gold Cup Oak, because of acorns' yellow cups.

**INTERIOR LIVE OAK** (to 75 ft.) is rare in Yosemite, though it is a common tree of the foothills. The leaves are shiny dark green, lighter beneath, and the margins are smooth or have small teeth. Acorns tapered, deep-set in scaly brown cups.

**BIGLEAF MAPLE** (to 50 ft.) has large leaves, sometimes 12 in. across. Foliage turns bright yellow in autumn. Grows in shady, moist places. Winged seeds to 1.5 in. long.

**CALIFORNIA-LAUREL** (to 60 ft.), also called Oregon Myrtle and Pepperwood, has pungent, evergreen leaves. In Yosemite, it is usually a small tree growing in moist places up to 5,000 ft.

**PACIFIC DOGWOOD** (to 40 ft.) is covered with white "blossoms" in May and June. In autumn, the leaves turn bright red as do clusters of red seeds. Grows along streams in moist places to about 5,000 ft.

**REDBUD** (to 20 ft.) actually more purple than red, blooms early in spring in the high foothills. It is Yosemite's most eye-catching shrub. The bright green, nearly round leaves do not appear until after the flowers.

**WESTERN AZALEA** (to 10 ft.), a rhododendron, fills the summer air with fragrance. Grows in dense clumps in moist places mostly between 3,000 and 7,000 ft. Whitish-pink flowers have yellow throats. Leaves group at ends of branches.

**CALIFORNIA BUCKEYE** (to 20 ft.) is a foothill tree, common along roads leading into the Park from the west. Its light-green leaves stand out among the darker foliage of other plants. White flowers are in clusters up to 8 in. long. Large seeds remain on tree after leaves fall.

**WESTERN CHOKECHERRY**, usually a shrub, occasionally grows to 20 ft., has dark green leaves lighter on underside; flowers white and in clusters. Bitter, berry-like purple fruits eaten by many birds.

**SWEETSHRUB**, or Spice Bush (to 10 ft.), is a showy shrub with magnolia-sized leaves. Crushed twigs are fragrant, from this the shrub receives its name. The dark purple flowers have a vinegar smell. Grows in foothills and up to about 4,000 ft.

**MOUNTAIN MISERY (to 18 in.)** is sometimes called Kit-kit-dizze, or Bear Clover. It grows in a low, solid mat in forests. Mountain Misery has white, roselike flowers, finely divided leaves, and a pungent odor. The Indians steeped its leaves for medicine.

**CEANOTHUS (to 10 ft.)** is a common Sierran genus of shrubs, including Buck Brush, Deer Brush and Snow Brush. The clusters of pungent, lilac-like flowers are white or light blue. Mahala Mat is a prostrate form with blue flowers.

**POISON OAK** has shiny, prominently veined leaves, always in groups of three. They turn red in the fall. Poison Oak's branching stalks may be short or in dense high clumps or climbing, like vines, on trees. Beware of this annoying plant!

**MANZANITA (to 10 ft.)** one of the most attractive of California shrubs, has twisted branches and trunk, shiny red bark and bell-shaped flowers. Six species grow in Yosemite region. Manzanita means "little apple," referring to the small green fruit.

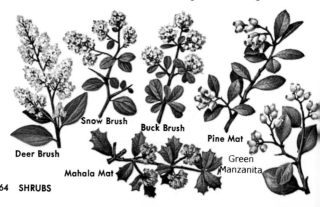

Snow Brush

Buck Brush

Pine Mat

Deer Brush

Mahala Mat

Green Manzanita

Lupine growing in Wawona Meadows

**WILDFLOWERS** are profuse in the foothills in spring-time, in the mountain meadows in early summer, and in the high Sierra in late summer and early fall. A few of the common species are described.

**LUPINE** flowers (about 50 species in Calif.) are usually blue or purple with white, though Stivers' Lupine is yellow and pink. Handlike leaves are green or silver gray. Bush Lupine may grow to 8 ft. tall; most kinds are a foot tall or less.

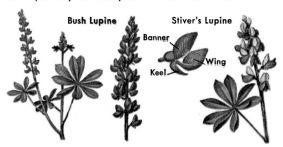

Bush Lupine

Stiver's Lupine

Banner

Wing

Keel

**CALIFORNIA POPPY** (to 20 in.), the state flower, has four triangular petals, usually golden orange, which close at night. Its leaves are finely divided, like a carrot's. Often makes a solid orange blanket over foothill fields and hillsides.

**BRODIAEA** are foothill wildflowers. Common Brodiaea, one of several species in Yosemite, has deep-blue flower clusters on ends of 12 to 15 in. stems. Blooms in spring. Golden Brodiaea flowers, which bloom in summer, are yellow. The leaves are basal and grasslike.

**CORN LILY** (to 6 ft.), sometimes mistaken for Skunk Cabbage, has thick stalks and large, heavily veined leaves. The small, greenish-white flowers grow thickly at the ends of branching stalks.

**COW PARSNIP**, often growing to 6 ft., is a showy plant in Yosemite meadows. The stems are stiff and hollow. Its whitish flowers grow in clusters on branches at tops of heavy stalks. Leaves are large and flat, resembling maple leaves. Said to be poisonous to cattle.

**EVENING PRIMROSE** has large yellow flowers that open in early evening and bloom all night on stalks up to 6 ft. tall. They are pollinated by large sphinx moths that hover as they feed from the flowers. Evening Primrose is a common flower in Yosemite Valley.

Golden Brodiaea

California Poppy

Corn Lily

Common Brodiaea

Cow Parsnip

Evening Primrose

Lupine and Indian Paint Brush brighten
a stream near Sunrise High Sierra Camp.

Shooting Stars predominate near
Bridalveil Creek.

Cow Parsnips front a Red Fir
forest above Badger Pass.

**MONKEY FLOWER**, or Mimulus, has five-lobed, inch-long yellow flowers, with purple or brown spots in the throat. Many kinds grow in the Sierra, from foothills to over 10,000 ft., usually in moist places.

**SNOWPLANT** (to 18 in.) is one of Yosemite's showiest plants with shiny red asparagus-like stalks and bell-shaped flowers. Snowplant grows singly or in clusters, often close to melting snow, from 4,000 to 7,000 ft.

**INDIAN PAINTBRUSH**, or Castilleja, flowers are in dense spikes, usually red though some are yellow or orange. Flowers are clustered at ends of stems that may be 12 in. long. Indian Paintbrush grows from the foothills to over 11,000 ft.

**MINER'S LETTUCE** leaves were eaten by miners and by Indians. Tiny white flowers grow at ends of long stems (up to 12 in.). Leaves, to half-dollar size, form collars below blossoms. Plants grow low, prefer shade. Common in Yosemite Valley.

**ELEPHANT HEADS** (to 12 in.) are found in high, wet meadows. They have small reddish flowers, each with a tiny trunk and ears, clustered thickly on the stalks. The curved trunks may grow to 0.5 in. long.

**SHOOTING STARS** (to 20 in.) give a purple color to many of the high meadows. The long petals point backward, somewhat suggesting a meteor's path. The leaves grow at the bases of the slender stems.

**PRIDE OF THE MOUNTAINS** has bright red, tubular flowers. It grows low, in rocky places from 5,000 to 10,000 ft. Other Penstemons grow in Yosemite including the blue-flowered Whorled Penstemon.

**LEOPARD LILY** (to 12 in.) likes moist places and grows at elevations up to 9,000 ft. Flowers droop at top of stalk, are bright orange-red with purple spots. The less-common Washington Lily has white flowers that turn purple as they age.

**HEATHERS** (to 12 in.) grow near the crest of the Sierra. Red Heather grows in clumps, blooms early in summer. Its flowers are in terminal clusters. White Heather has bell-shaped, drooping white flowers, grows along streams and on rocky ledges.

**FERNS** of more than 30 kinds grow in the Sierra. Some are lush and green and grow in moist places. Others, like Bracken, prefer open meadows where they add golden color in fall. The most difficult to identify are the

**FIVE-FINGER FERN** (to 2 in.) branches near the top, commonly into five smaller branches. The flattened leaflets are notched at tip and are opposite on the branches. This fern grows in cool, moist crevices.

**LADY FERN** (to 4 ft.) grows from 4,000 to 8,000 ft. in the Sierra. The broad fronds are on short stems. Leaf forms vary, may be deeply notched. The spore bodies are moon-shaped. Often grown in gardens.

**CALIFORNIA MAIDENHAIR** (to 24 in.) is a delicate fern with slender black stalks. The fan-shaped leaflets have spore clusters along their edges. Grows in shaded habitats, from the foothills to 3,000 ft.

**CALIFORNIA WOOD FERN** (to 3 ft.) often grows in open, semi-dry places from 2,000- to over 5,000-ft. elevation. Its evergreen fronds have stout stems. Small spore covers under leaflets are kidney-shaped.

several blue-gray Cliff Brakes that grow in dry, rocky places at medium to high altitudes.

Ferns reproduce by tiny spores formed on undersides of the fronds. Spores may travel long distances on wind.

**SIERRA CLIFF BRAKE** grows in dry, rocky habitats up to 11,000 ft. Sierra Cliff Brake has brittle, brown stalks, and the clumps of grayish fronds may be 9 or 10 in. tall. Several related species grow in the Sierra.

**SWORD FERN** (to 4 ft.), often used in decorations has shiny green tapering fronds. It prefers moist, shady places, from foothills to above 7,000 ft. Round spore bodies are in rows on margins of frond segments.

**GIANT CHAIN FERN,** or Woodwardia, largest California fern, has fronds often more than 6 ft. tall. It requires continual moisture. Leaflets notched, nearly to midrib, and oblong bodies form a chain along midvein.

**BRACKEN** (to 4 ft.) is the most common fern of Yosemite Valley in open meadows and forests, but is found in many parts of the Sierra. Fronds grow on individual stalks. Indians used roots for food and baskets.

Horsetail

Quillwort

Selaginella

Moss

Sulphur-bracket fungus

Lichens

Wolf Lichen

**HORSETAILS AND CLUB MOSSES** are primitive fern ancestors. Common Horsetail and the Scouring Rushes look like reeds and grow in wet places. Silica in their stems made them useful to pioneers for polishing pots and pans. Of the four genera of Club Mosses, two grow in the Sierra. *Selaginella* is the common Resurrection Plant. The Quillwort grows in wet places.

**MOSSES** may be confused with lichens, but lichens are dry, often crusty to the touch, while mosses normally grow in wet places and are soft and green. Some of the 40 kinds of mosses native to the Sierra do dry up and close during warm weather. Mosses are primitive, produce spores in capsules.

**FUNGI** include mushrooms, toadstools, puffballs and some that grow like shelves on trees. Some, like the Sulphur-bracket Fungus, may be bright yellow; others are red, black or pure white. Fungi lack chlorophyll; hence they draw their food from other plants or animals, either dead or living. Some mushrooms are edible; others are deadly poisonous.

**LICHENS** are small, primitive plants. Some are bright red, yellow or green; others are gray or dark brown. Lichens grow in three distinct forms: *crustose*, or crustlike, which are pressed so tightly against rocks or bark that plants look like spilled paint; *foliose*, that look much like peeling paint; and *fruticose*, which look like moss.

Visitors with Ranger at Glacier Point

## WHAT TO SEE AND DO IN THE PARK

**YOSEMITE ROADS** are well maintained but they are mountain roads so drive with caution. Some, like the Tioga Road across the Sierra, are closed by snow in winter. Study the map you received when you entered the park or talk to a ranger. Stop and look. Take your time as you drive through the park. Much of the most beautiful scenery is along the way rather than at a particular destination. Many turnouts have explanatory signs, or numbered posts to match the self guiding booklet, *Yosemite Road Guide,* available at museums and visitor centers.

**VISIT A MUSEUM, VISITOR CENTER, OR HISTORY CENTER.**

Exhibits and audio visual presentations will help you understand features of the park and where they are located (see map, page 6). These include:

*Yosemite Valley Visitor Center*

How Yosemite Valley was formed. *Spirit of Yosemite* film shown frequently. Information, maps, exhibits. Open all year.

*Yosemite Museum*

Frequent programs about nature. Gift shop. Open all year.

*Indian Village*

Located behind the museum. The story of the Valley's original residents. Open all year.

*Pioneer Yosemite History Center*

Yosemite in stagecoach days. Open all Year.

*Mariposa Grove Museum*

The Giant Sequoias. Information, exhibits, books. Closed in winter.

Rangers Lead Bird Walks

*Glacier Point Overlook*
Geology and the High Sierra.
Ranger walks, evening programs. Closed in winter.

*Tuolumne Meadows Visitor Center*
The High Sierra. Trail information, maps, books. Closed in winter.

## RANGER-LED ACTIVITIES
are frequent in many parts of the park in summer. These include nature walks and hikes, museum talks and campfire programs. Check bulletin boards or inquire at museums or visitor centers for times.

Junior Rangers

## JUNIOR RANGERS
Program for youngsters meets in summer at Happy Isles Nature Center. Rangers explain nature and the park and present awards. Check bulletin boards or information desks for meeting times.

Nature Walk

## LOOK FOR WATERFALLS
At their best in late spring and early summer, most are easily seen from the roads and trails (see maps, pages 5,6,7). Many, including Yosemite Falls, become dry as High Country snows melt.

## INDIAN DEMONSTRATONS

Occasional programs behind the Yosemite Museum may include a basket weaver demonstrating her skills and a staff member explaining food, clothing and way of life of the Miwok Indians who once lived in Yosemite Valley.

## GIANT SEQUIOA TREES

Three groves. The largest and best known is the Mariposa Grove, about 5 miles from South Entrance, on the road to Fresno (Highway 41). Here was the Wawona Tunnel Tree through which you could drive your car before it toppled in early 1969. Mariposa Grove Museum is in the midst of the big trees. Tuolumne and Merced groves are on the northwest side of the park, near the Big Oak Flat Road. All access roads are usually closed by snow in winter; hence the museum is closed also.

## FISHING

is legal in the park. A State of California license is required (see page 50). Some streams may be restricted to fly fishing or use of barbless hooks. Some High Country lakes have been stocked by dropping fingerling trout from airplanes. For regulations ask at park headquarters or ask a ranger.

Indian Basket Weaver

Fishing in Yosemite

75

**TRAILS TO HIKE** put you close to the scenery and wildlife. Before you start, remember these rules: (1) Never hike alone; (2) Stay on the trail---don't take shortcuts; (3) Tell someone your destination. Many trails are closed in winter. Respect the signs---they are for your safety. Topographic maps of the park and valley are available at museums and studios.

**MORE THAN 200 MILES OF ROADS** are open for driving in the park except during winter when the High Country is closed by snow. A useful booklet is *Yosemite Road Guide,* available at museums and studios. Its text is keyed to numbered wooden posts at the roadside describing features. Check the map you received when you entered the park for road information. Glacier Point gives excellent views of Merced Canyon, and Yosemite Falls, and the High Country beyond. Reached by a good mountain road (see map, page 5). Some 6 miles up from the Chinquapin junction is a turnoff to the Badger Pass Ski Area. In winter the road is only open this far. In summer Badger Pass Meadow is a beautiful wildflower garden. When you reach Glacier Point, park your car and walk to the overlook exhibit for spectacular views of Yosemite Valley 3000 feet below as well as Half Dome and the peaks of the High Sierra beyond.

**PIONEER YOSEMITE HISTORY CENTER:** a covered bridge, stage coaches and wagons, and early buildings. In summer there are stagecoach rides and "living history" demonstrators depicting the way of life in early days. Just north of historic Wawona Hotel. The covered bridge, visible upstream from the bridge across the main road shows the way.

**TRY DIFFERENT SEASONS** Visitors who must gear trips to summer vacations find Yosemite crowded when they arrive. In other seasons there is more beauty and much more space. Yosemite is open all year and is a popular winter sports area. Major roads are kept open in winter excepting the Tioga Road across the Sierra.

**WILD ANIMALS** of many kinds and sizes are native to the park, including deer and bear. Approach with caution. Take photographs from a safe distance. Keep children back and do not attempt to feed the animals. Booklets to help you identify mammals, birds, reptiles and other animals are available at museums and studios.

DEVILS POSTPILE

Cooling lava from an ancient volcano shrank to form the many-sided rock columns of the Devils Postpile, a National Monument on the east side of the Sierra Nevada not far from Yosemite (see map). Several similar formations are world-famous, including Fingal's Cave (Scotland), the Giant's Causeway (Ireland) and the Palisades along the Hudson River in New York.

In the Devils Postpile, dozens of smooth-sided columns are fitted together in a way that gives the appearance of a carefully engineered project rather than a casual event of nature.

Geologists say that the lava which became the Postpile was highly fluid when it was forced onto the earth's surface. As it cooled and shrank, cracks formed at right angles to lines of stress and made the columns. Some of

Hexagonal columns

these are more than 50 feet high and over one foot in diameter. A majority are six-sided, but they vary from four to seven sides.

A short path leads to the top of the Postpile. There you can look across the tops of the many-sided columns. You can also see the smooth surface made by a glacier which scraped over the Postpile after it had cooled, polishing the rock with the abrasives carried with the ice. Many posts have fallen as broken rubble at the base of the upright columns. Expansion and contraction from weather and the effect of water freezing in cracks have played a part, but such action takes thousands of years. Much more rapid would have been its destruction from a proposal to blast the Postpile into the San Joaquin River, to form a dam for generating electric power for mining. Far-sighted men opposed this request to destroy the Postpile, and in 1911, President Taft signed a bill forming the Devils Postpile National Monument. The area is administered today by the National Park Service, co-operating with the U.S. Forest Service.

At Rainbow Falls, at the southern end of the monument, the Middle Fork of the San Joaquin River drops 140 feet over rock similar to the Postpile. The afternoon sun striking the falls often makes a beautiful rainbow. Devils Postpile is reached by traveling 19 miles from Highway 395. During the summer rangers conduct nature walks and hold campfire programs for visitors. Snows cover the Postpile and close the road in winter.

**INDEX**